NORTH OF GRIMSBY

Great Grimsby. Pop 95,000

Famous Alumni:-

Grim (Hence Grims-by – BY being a Danish word for settlement or Dwelling) and Havelok the Dane

John Whitgift (Archbishop of Canterbury 1583) House was recently a cycle shop.

Freddie Frinton – Actor "Dinner for One" is the most repeated tv show in Germany, and is on TV every New Years Eve.

Rod Temperton -Worked in a Grimsby Fish Finger Factory and wrote "Thriller" for Michael Jackson.

After a traumatic delivery, I entered this world in March 1963, and first lived in

A small terraced house, off Cromwell Rd. It was close to a public house euphemistically called "The Market Hotel", which had a grand pub sign on a round plinth and sold the locally brewed Hewitt Ales. Due to enlightened times, the sign has disappeared, and the pub is now a Tesco Express, with the adjoining beer off the delightfully name Fruitolinka polish food store.

What I remember about the house was that it was at the bottom of a dead end street, had 2 bedrooms, and an outside toilet, and a privet hedge at the front. There was a small bush in the garden, which dad said was poisonous if I ate the berries. It was very near the countryside, as my dad regularly took me to see the local sheep. It was only a few years later that I discovered this was in fact the local abattoir. Due to progress, this is now a small housing estate. Unfortunately, there is no homage to the previous use, I rather like the idea of Offal Avenue or Tripe Terrace. It's called Finchley Court, which may be a homage to Maggie Thatcher, who in some people's eyes, was a cow.

Opposite the Market Hotel, just before the viaduct, the No 2 bus stopped. The local buses where a distinctive blue and cream livery, made by either Daimler or AEC (Associated Equipment Company), and had a bus conductor. They were usually full., and contained signs advising "no spitting", with smoking upstairs. Sadly, most local bus companies have disappeared, and unique liveries replaced by the corporate colours of multi nationals such as Stagecoach.

Very close to the bus stop, was an area that used to be the Cattle Market, hence The Market Hotel, and for a short while the May fun fair was there.

However, the reason for catching the No 2, was to visit my maternal great granny, who lived down the longest street in Grimsby, Weelsby St. In a typical 2 up, 2 down terrace, without a front garden. It didn't have much of a back yard either as I recall, mainly overgrown grass, weeds that had heads that stuck to you, which we called darts, and a corrugated dustbin. The families living in this area were closely linked to the Fishing Industry, as the local fish dock, with its imposing and grand Royal Dock Tower, was close by. Most men in the area had been to sea (many being lost) or worked on the fish docks in careers with such great names as Lumper, Filleter or Production Line Operative. Well known Frozen Food firms, such as Findus, Bird's-eye and Ross, employed thousands. Sadly, due to progress, no-one goes to sea, Lumpers don't exist, and the factories have mostly disappeared.

Memories of Granny Plastow are pretty threadbare. I know she was born in 1888, and I can remember that she always seemed to be in a bed in the front room, next to a coal fire, and something that was called a grate. I do remember often getting a blue riband wafer and a glass of Robinsons barley water. I think I preferred the Blue Riband. The Christmas before she died, Granny Plastow bought me a Dinky

Man from U. N. C. L. E. car where Ilya Kuryakin and Napoleon Solo would emerge to shoot anti American criminals. My nanna, Ivy, didn't live with Granny Plastow, but caught the No 10 bus to her house every day. My Mum always says Granny's tea was as weak as gnats piss. She carries on the Family tradition.

In July 1965, my brother Kevin Andrew North was born. I think Dad was at work, he was a lumper, working nights on the fish docks, and Nanna Tilling, the one who caught the No 10 every day, rang the Ambulance. The trips on the No2 to Granny Plastows' were replaced by riding shotgun on top of a Green and White Silver Cross perambulator. It was quite a walk, by passing the underground toilets in the old marketplace, and navigating one of the longest underpasses in England before we reached Weelsby Street. Grimsby also had one of the longest footbridges, spanning the many railways that served the fish docks. Now, an hourly service that goes as far as Manchester Airport, and a branch line to Barton upon Humber are all that pass under it.

I seem to remember Kev was quite a chubby child, who did not like having his photo taken. About this time, I had a few friends who used to play in our garden. One grew up to be a well-known local butcher, there was another lad with the odd surname Melhuish, and a girl who apparently used to bite me. I bit her back one day and got a smack on the legs from my mum. And, she didn't eat the berries from the bush in the garden.

We had no car, no fridge, a 16-inch black and white telly, on which I may have watched a mix of Andy Pandy, The Flowerpot Men, Camberwick Green , featuring Windy Miller, and a small girl with a model clown playing noughts and crosses. I looked through geometrically shaped windows, descibed by Brian Cant -the doyen of kids telly in the sixties,(who also provided the voices for Camberwick Green and Trumpton) and remember Miss Rosalind, who could see people through her magic mirror, in Romper Room. She never saw Tony ! (probably due to the tv hierarchy insisting that she say Anthony). A rabbit called Dylan, who appeared to have been on wacky baccy, and a curious creature with a spring for legs, known as Zebedee, would often appear just before bedtime. I may have had strange dreams !

One day, a red and white sign, bearing the inscription "For Sale Jackson and Green "(I don't think Preston was on there) appeared in the garden, and soon we were on our way to our new House. It was August 1967. Scott McKenzie was No1, but the Grimsby Lumper, his Fish Finger producing wife, and their 2 young sons certainly didn't have flowers in their hair.

Chapter 2

Limber Vale

I seem to remember Dad walking us from the bus stop, (probably the No 4), down Grange Walk, to No 9 Limber Vale. Quite a posh name for a small nondescript thoroughfare on the west side of Grimsby. But this was a step up from Bowers Avenue and would be the home for the formative years of my life.

We had a Shed, which Dad initially parked his Vespa in. (He wasn't a mod; I just think he got it cheap). The house was an "end terrace", virtually a semi in mam's eyes. A passage separated us from the Short family, where Mr. Short, who was also a Lumper, lovingly molly coddled his pride and joy, a BSA motorbike and side car. Dad painted the outside in Jonquil Yellow with Home Charm paint from Grandways.

We now had 2 and a half bedrooms, a driveway an inside toilet, and a gas convection heater at the bottom of the stairs. We bought a Hoover fridge, and got a 19 inch TV (UHF and VHF) from Rediffusion. It even showed Anglia TV! Fred Dinage did the football on Yorkshire TV, and Keith Macklin over on Anglia. Each ITV channel had its own logo, my favourite was the Anglia knight rotating to the sound of Handels water music ! We had gone up in the world.!

After Christmas 1967, I was taken by my mam, to Lawson and Stockdale where she bought me a grey blazer, edged in Red, some grey shorts, grey socks with red stripes, and a pair of Tuf shoes. I was going to Worsley Infants School, named after the son of the Earl of Yarborough, who was probably the biggest land owner in the area. Egalitarianism was still in the wings!

I don't think I got off to the best of starts and cried as Mam said goodbye at Worsley school gate. She would be there to take me home at dinner (lunch hadn't been invented in the North household), and back in the afternoon. If I had been at the Nursery, I would have got an hour's sleep.

Strangely, Worsley school, whose Headmistress Miss Bean flew Lancaster bombers in the war, adopted a reading scheme called I. T. A. This meant it was phonetic rather than alphabetic, so, if I took a book home to read, Mam and Dad didn't have a bloody clue.

However, every time you completed one of Janet and John's stories, after reading a few lines to Miss Bean, you were allowed to take 2 smarties out of a tin in her study.

I never liked Mrs. Webster. I think this may have contributed to my nervous weak bladder, compounded by the fact that Worsley's equivalent of Miss Trunchbull would never let me go to the toilet. This led to me occasionally weeing my pants. It also led to my Dad visiting Mrs. Webster and tearing a strip of her. Well, more likely asking her politely to allow me to go to the loo when I put my hand up.

America put a man on the moon, I got transferred to Mrs. Watsons class. Mrs. Watson had the honour of organizing the annual "Worsley carnival queen "contest (this was the sixties after all, and Worsley had merrily jumped on the Eric Morley bandwagon), and I was asked to nominate a potential queen. The person I nominated was a bit weird, and only secured one vote, mine!

At the end of the swinging sixties, which probably never swung that much in Grimsby, and at the time when the free and liberal population had made Rolf Harris's Two little boys the last No 1 of the decade, I turned down the opportunity to play Prince Charming in the school play, in order that I could dress up as a footballer and sing "Blue is the colour", or maybe "Back Home " My nascent acting career was nipped in the bud at the first Hurdle.

I reckon 1969 was also the year we went on our first family holiday. Dad had passed his Driving test and bought a pretty unreliable 1962 white Ford Anglia. Somehow, it got us to a Hoseasons holiday park in Hemsby, Norfolk. (England not Virginia). We hired a boat (a rowing boat), and visited Gt Yarmouth. Also, a weirdly named pub called "The Eels Foot Inn ". Zager and Evans were singing about the Year 2525, but we were still in the 1960's. However, we had made it to Hoseasons, and we were still alive.

The following year, the Anglia had gone to the great scrapyard in the sky, so we went to Blackpool on the Train (Changing at Manchester and Preston). A trip up the Tower, and a Tram to Fleetwood I can remember, as well as the illuminations, and a trip to see a well-known comedian called Al Read, who had a great catchphrase, "Right, Monkey"! ; but Dad had a real Ace up his sleeve.

Louis Tussauds was a second-class version of its famous Matriarchal waxworks, and it had second rate models of the Queen, Harold Wilson, Richard Nixon and maybe the Beatles, although they may just been melted down to help created the unsuccessful 1970 England World cup team. I have vague memories of grainy colour TV pictures, and an excitable David Coleman annunciating exotic names such as Jaaarzinho, Rivelinooo, and of course Pelaaay ! (Pele). I also think Peter Bonnetti had a mare. I vaguely remember watching the final, and for those of you watching in black and white, Brazil are in the yellow, and Italy in blue. Brazil won 4-1, in the heat of the Azteca stadium, in a game often regarded as the best ever World Cup Final (discuss!).

However, all that was forgotten, as Derek North decided to take his 2 sons, aged 5 & 7 into the "Chamber of Horrors". Dracula, a fatal car crash and an Indian scalping a cowboy weren't exactly U certificate material. I shit myself, and Derek got a verbal volley from Mother.

To make it worse, we were staying in the attic of a dingy B&B, and so that night, I was woken every hour by a man in a cloak, about to plunge his fangs into my neck. My first nightmare! I wished the Magic Roundabout dreams would override it.

Chapter 3.

Blundell Park, it's one of the oldest football grounds in the country, is actually in Cleethorpes, and to be honest, has not changed that much since I first visited towards the end of 1970. My first actual visit to a football ground was in the aftermath of my visit from the Lord of darkness. Dad took me to Maine Rd to watch Manchester City v West Bromwich Albion in Division 1 of the English League.
Household names of the day were on show, such as Colin Bell, Mike Sumerbee, and Francis Lee. Jeff Astle played for WBA, and I think City won 4- 1. Jeff sadly died of dementia caused by heading too many rock-hard footballs, but in later life did enjoy a brief stint as a singer on Skinner and Badiel's Fantasy Football. Francis Lee went on to be a toilet roll magnate, and apparently employed Peter Kay.

Mam and Kev went shopping in Manchester, mam possibly buying some maternity wear, as she was pregnant again.

My trips to Blundell started to become regular, and armed with a milk crate, me and dad would get a lift off Johnny Gibbins, who had a lime green Morris Marina.

To start with, I used to stand on the inside of the Pitch perimeter, running on every time Matt Tees, Stuart Brace et al scored.

Lawrie McMenemy, an ex-guard turned football manager had arrived from Doncaster, to try and save GTFC ignominiously falling out the League. He didn't have any money to spend and crowds had dwindled to about 2,000. Fast forward to 2021, and its deja-vu (apart from, due to covid, the 2,000 fans).

Anyway, Lawrie, who mam thought was " a bit of alright " got the team gelling, and on an unforgettable night in May 1971, town beat Exeter City in front of a crowd of around 23,000

(health and safety would have gone berserk today!)

And town won the 4th division title. Mam got a final sight of McMenemy at the Civic reception, although

Laurie can't have been that impressed as he buggered off to Southampton. We were on holiday in Mablethorpe when it was announced, at Mablethorpe Chalet Park. Some people were going Pontinental , but a 20 mile trip down the Lincolnshire coast in a sky blue Ford Cortina (HLY 2C), was good enough for the Norths.

Dad was also keen on Horse Racing. Every Saturday we would sit in silence as we watched the racing on BBC or ITV. (Peter O'Sullievan on BBC, which was part of Grandstand, or John Oaksey and Brough Scott on ITV). The Grand National was a big day. Dad would allow us all a 50p ew, as well as doing a sweepstake, and I do remember having some money on horses such as Grey Sombrero and Glandford Brigg, as well as the occasional winner such as Lucius and Corbierre. I never backed Red Rum.

Concord was big news. The sleek looking, delta wing supersonic aircraft was an Anglo-French triumph, and apparently made hell of a noise when taking off. However, the decibel level was nothing compared to those that emanated from number 344 Convamore Rd every Tuesday and Friday.

This was the home of Lily North, my paternal Nanna. We would catch the No 4 bus to Durban Rd, and alight opposite a small, old fashioned bakery which sold delicious, warm bread buns and fruit cakes. If we were lucky, mam would buy some, and they would still be warm when we reached Nannas.

The Cacophony of Noise would often hit you as soon as you walked through the front door. Unlike Weelsby St, Nannas house did have a small front garden, and the head of an old king above the porch.

Nanna, and my 4 aunties would partake in a verbal jousting match, the rules of which seemed to be.

1. Talk as loud as you can
2. If anyone is talking louder than you, talk louder.
3. Never, ever, take a breath, as that was the equivalent of being winded by a lance.

4. Don't listen to what anyone else says, it's your opinion that counts
5. Be careful what you say to Audrey and Hilda, Nana's neighbours.
6. The loser goes to Arnolds chip shop to get dinner in.
7. In the end, Nanna is always right.

Nanna North lived in the same house for 60 years., but she would often come to Limber Vale, to "babymind " us.
Since January 1971, at the time of George Harrisons "My Sweet Lord " Darren Michael North had joined the family. Mam and Dad's hope for a Girl hadn't materialized, and the anticipated Jamie Spencer North had been changed at the last minute by mam, who could be a bit spontaneous, to Darren Michael. Me and Kev chose Michael.
He was always a chubby baby and slept in the bedroom that in these days would have been called the en -suite to the master bedroom. But

as en -suite wouldn't enter the North vocabulary for another 30 years, we called it the Little Bedroom.

Anyway, back to Nanna staying on Saturday Nights. Mam and Dad often went out on Saturday nights to the Hainton Recreation Club, where a "turn" would be on, and where women were only allowed on a Saturday night. Progress now means they can now visit any day of the week.

Other times Dad might get a bus trip to Caenby Corner or the Chestnuts at Glentham. A couple of times they went as far as the Batley Variety club to see stars of the day such as the American Singers Neil Sedaka and Johnny Matthis. Dad missed Johnny, as he was walking the streets of Batley attempting to sober up.

Nights with Nanna were interesting. We would eat matchmakers and watch a series on ITV called "Thriller "or the totally un-PC Black and

White minstrel show. I remember one particular night when we couldn't get the gas fire to light. I decided to make a newspaper taper and got a light from our New World gas cooker.

I lit the fire in the room, but on discarding the taper into the rooms litter bin, managed to set that ablaze.

We managed to put out the fire, it may even have been with nannas snowball and lemonade. School was out, according to Alice Cooper.

Chapter 3.

Most people in Grimsby had a connection with the fishing industry. In the seventies, Grimsby was one of the largest fishing ports in the world, and a multitude of trawlers could be seen if you visited the fish docks. As my dad worked as a lumper on the fish docks, he would often take us "down dock" to have a wander round. A lumper was the local name for the large group of workers who would unload the trawlers overnight, in order that fish was ready for the morning fish market. This took place on the Pontoon, where varieties of fish from the seas around Iceland, Norway, Russia and Scotland where auctioned. Cod, Haddock, Plaice, Monkfish and the massive Halibuts could be seen. On any given day, you could see dozens of boats tied up on the North Wall, awaiting fresh provisions before setting off again to their Northern Fishing grounds. Most where black in colour, with funnels indicating which company the Trawlers belonged to.

Names such as Northern, Boston, Ross and Consolidated owned the vessels, and often the company name would precede the moniker of the trawler. Ross ships had a group named after cats, such as Tiger, Puma, Civet, whilst the Consols had a fleet named after Football teams, so on any given day on the Dock, you could see Everton, Arsenal, Spurs and Grimsby Town, to name a few!

Dad would often take us on the pontoon and dare us to stand as close as possible to the edge of the fish docks as we could. He had an odd sense of humour !

My Uncle John was worked his way up from a lowly deckie learner on trawlers, to the role of skipper. He was a big man, with a big reputation, but in those days, Skippers were a revered breed of men, and many crews were loyal to a good skipper. This was probably due to the fact that the more fish that was caught, the more money was earned.

Deep Sea fishing was an unusual profession, which entailed ships sailing for distant waters, mainly around Iceland, fishing for 3 weeks, and then returning to port for 3 or 4 days.

Not surprisingly, many would enjoy their time ashore to the full, and it was a boom time for the Towns pubs and shops, especially around Freeman Street, which was a main thoroughfare close to the fish dock entrance.

At its northern end was Riby Square, the town's well-known red-light district. Fishermen worked hard and played hard, and the town often reflected this ethos. Money earned was quickly spent, and many flash cars and large houses were bought on the proceeds of a "good trip", and financial advice was not a high priority.

Amazingly, after the decline of deep sea fishing, mainly due to Iceland imposing a 200 mile exclusion zone around its coast,(in a series of disputes called the Cod Wars, which the UK, lost, possibly due to the US having a strategic

Air Base there at the height of the Cold War.)
The Fishermen were unceremoniously thrown
on the scrap heap, and deemed as "casual
labour", so that redundancy payments didn't
have to be paid.
Today, the fish docks are a sad shadow of what
they were 50 years ago, and impressive
buildings, such as the Ice Factory are almost
derelict.

However, growing up at the tail end of the
town's fishing prosperity must have left a lasting
impression, as I once wrote a fictional novel
based on the industry, for a competition in the
Grimsby Evening Telegraph. It Didn't win, so I've
put it in print here! You might enjoy it!

THE KING OF ALBANIA Tony North.

January 1976.

The dying chords of Bohemian Rhapsody crackled over the radio, as Alan "Fluff" Freeman announced another week at number one.

"Paterson, are you just going to sit there and listen to that rubbish, or are you coming down dock with me, before it's too late? "

DCI Bert Shrewsbury was in a foul mood, and Paterson was in the firing line. The recent string of vicious assaults in the West Marsh area of town culminating in a terrible murder a couple of days ago, had the local tight knit community in twitchy mood, and Charlie Edison, well known hack on the Grimsby Evening Telegraph as well as eccentric raconteur on BBC radio Humberside was not giving him any slack, with a string of barely disguised digs at the ineptitude of the local constabulary.

DS Graham Paterson grabbed his coat and ran to the Morris Minor squad car parked in the police compound, whilst a wheezing DCI Shrewsbury struggled to keep up. Thirty years of a plus 40 a day habit smoking Senior Service fags had taken its toll.

Shrewsbury eventually got his breath back and motioned to Paterson to get into the driving seat.

"Why the hell are we using this heap of crap" Bert asked

"Not sure, but someone said the Jags been nicked!" Shrewsbury and Paterson sped of (metaphorically speaking), and the Morris squealed as they turned into Freeman Street and passed the local ABC cinema. "JAWS" was currently being shown there.

"Have you seen it sir? "Enquired Paterson.

"Nope, the last time I went to the flick's it was a Night to Remember, and I don't mean with me and the missus" Shrewsbury replied.

Five minutes later Bert and Paterson dragged themselves out of the Morris, parked under the shadow of the Dock Tower, and looked forlornly out into the muddy waters of the Humber.

The trawler, GY 642, King of Albania, had just exited the lock gates on a 21-day trip to Iceland.

"Sod it" the two men yelled in unison.

10 Days later

"Icelandic gunships have cut the nets of 2 British Trawlers in the most recent skirmishes of the Icelandic Cod War "Grainy black and white TV pictures showing the Icelandic gun boat Thor approaching GY 642, accompanied the cut glass announcers accent of BBC evening news presenter, Peter Woods.

Pat Hewitt had seen it all before. Like most families in the town, her's was steeped in fishing tradition. Grandfather, Father and now Husband, had all earned their living from deep sea fishing, and the family had, like many in the town, suffered tragedy. Her Uncle had perished at sea in 1954, when the trawler Laforey sank off the coast of Norway.

This Cod war business was not the first skirmish over fishing grounds between Britain and Iceland. The first "war" was in 1958 when the limit was extended to 12 miles around the coast, earlier in the seventies when it was pushed to 50 miles, and now The Icelanders wanted to push the limit to 200 miles. If successful, this would almost signal the demise of the British Deep-Sea Fishing industry, and the hardy souls risking their lives to get food back on the tables of Britain were in angry mood.

Pat shouted to her two children to come into the front room "Look, that's Dads Ship on Telly".

The Day Before

Joe Taylor stood in the wheelhouse of GY 642, King of Albania, he had spent all his working career fishing, from deckie learner to Skipper, but instinctively knew that this could be one of his last trip to these Fishing Grounds that he had fished most of his life.
His mate, Frank Charrington was a hard-working brute of a man, who could keep the crew in check, but had a vicious temper. He also liked a few beers.

Vic Hewitt had sailed with Taylor on many occasions and Taylor saw him as a reliable sort, who could fillet fish at unimaginable speed. Taylor and Hewitt had had some great trips together, and between them had earned quite a bit of money.

Alan Tetley was the newest member of the crew, and as a newly qualified radio operator this was his first sojourn on the King of Albania.

There was another reasonably new face on the vessel, a Dane called Sven Nielsen, and Joe Taylor was not keen on him. He didn't mix well with the other crew members, and his presence led to an uneasy air around the decks of the vessel. He was, however, a bloody good cook!!

Finally, Joe considered the Boat. The King of Albania had seen better days, but not many. Owned by Kings Trawlers Ltd, King of Albania was the runt of the litter. Sister ships King of Greece, King of Sweden and King of Norway were newer and bigger vessels, and the King of Albania was the oldest and smallest of the quartet.

Its black hull was showing great signs of deterioration, and it was a miracle that this ageing rust bucket was still afloat. But not for much longer, after this 3-week journey, the ship was to be retired and broken up for scrap. Joe and his crew knew finding another ship would not be that easy.

12 Days earlier.

"I reckon we know our murderer" yelled Shrewsbury.

Paterson looked startled as Bert stormed into the room, as he had once again been captivated by Bohemian Rhapsody, still playing on the Radio.

"Who do you reckon it is then "Paterson enquired. Shrewsbury had been doing his homework. The two violent attacks prior to the murder had happened in early December 1975, and the one prior to that around late October. All the attacks had coincided with certain ships being in port, where their catches were un loaded by the towns army of Lumpers, before the ship returning to the North Wall where it would be re stocked before returning to the Icelandic fishing grounds.

One particular vessel had caught Shrewsbury's attention. GY 642, King of Albania, was in port during the attacks, so Bert had delved deeper into the list of crew on that vessel, as well as others in port at the times of the attacks. One name had made Bert investigate further, as Sven Nielsen, had only been in Town since late September, and had only sailed on this particular ship.

It transpired that Nielsen had been out drinking down Freeman St, the haunt of many of the towns Fishermen due to its close proximity to the Fish Docks, the night before New Year's Eve, 1975. Whilst in the Corporation Arms he had been playing Dominoes with some of the locals, and, had got steaming drunk.

On leaving the pub at around 10.30 he had been ranting about the right the Icelandic's had to their

Fishing grounds, and that he would kill anyone who thought otherwise. In the Early hours of New Year's Eve 1975, the body of a young woman, Jenny Mann, had been found in the car park opposite the Grimsby General Hospital in the West Marsh area of town. Her throat had been slit.

Jenny had worked as a prostitute, plying her trade around Riby Square, and had been seen talking to Nielsen shortly after he had left the "Corp". Residents close to the Hospital had heard a commotion around midnight, and one of them had gone to investigate what was going on. He discovered Jenny struggling for life, bleeding profusely from a large gash across her throat. She died in his arms, and a well-worn filleting knife was found beside her. The resident swore he had seen a burly figure running off in the direction of Top Town.

Shrewsbury and Paterson had arrived at the crime scene shortly after 1am; the only piece of evidence was the knife, which they would get SOCO's to check for dabs.

Shrewsbury's enquiries over the subsequent days had given him a pretty good idea that the man in the frame for the murder was a crew member of the King of Albania. Shrewsbury recalled that there had been a couple of similar attacks in Fleetwood, that had not been solved, and enquiries via colleagues at the Lancashire Constabulary had showed that a Dane called Sven Nielsen had sailed out of the port during 1975, and was in port when the attacks in Fleetwood had occurred.

Subsequent enquiries had discovered that Nielsen was not who he purported to be , and was in fact an Icelandic resident going by the name of Bjarne Sigurdsson, whose family where from Reykjavik, and some of them had been involved in the previous 2 Cod Wars. It turned out his mates in The Corporation knew him as the "Icelandic".

11 days later

Things were turning ugly off the Icelandic Coast. So far, there had been little incident involving GY 642, and Jack and the crew had probably been lulled into a false sense of security. Catches had so far been pretty good, and at this rate the ships final trip was going to be a reasonably profitable one.

The nets were winched in again, when suddenly, the reality of the conflict was too smack them in the face. The Icelandic Gunboat Thor appeared on the scene and headed straight towards The King of Albania.

Alan Tetley made radio contact with the fisheries protection vessel HMS Lowestoft, informing them that Thor was closing in, and an incident was likely.

As the Thor approached the King of Albania, shortly before the bulging cod end of the trawl had been winched aboard, the Thor cut through the warps of the nets, destroying the catch. On board the trawler, the hawser reeled back violently, and managed to glance a blow across Vince Hewitt's arm. Vince had become an unwitting casualty of the war.

Down in the radio room, Alan Tetley relayed a message back to the ship's owners, Kings Trawlers Ltd, that the nets had been cut and the catch lost. It would be the last ever message sent from GY 642, King of Albania.

3 Days later

"Queen there, who are still at number one with Bohemian Rhapsody" announced Charlie Edison on his weekly Radio Humberside talk show.

Being a resident of Grimsby, it was with great trepidation that Charlie introduced his next item.

"Fears are growing for the safety of the Trawler King of Albania, which has not made radio contact for 3 days ".

Charlie's mood matched that of the tight knit community of Grimsby, whose residents were expecting little good news about GY 642. The sombre atmosphere around town was tangible, and quite a few folks would know of someone on the missing vessel. The Billboards of The Grimsby Evening Telegraph, stationed at strategic positions around the area announced in funereal black ink

GRIMSBY TRAWLER-STILL MISSING.

A constant stream of family and friends visited the neat semi-detached house that Pat Hewitt and her family lived in, on the towns Willows Estate. The newly installed telephone had barely stopped ringing as well-meaning people rang to see if there was anything they could do.

Pat was putting on her brave face for the sake of her two children, but she realised that they knew something wasn't quite right. She comforted them the best she could, telling them Dad would soon be home, but her reassurances were rather shallow.

At the few precious times when she could find a bit of time on her own, she broke down.

A few days later, Bert Shrewsbury and Brian Paterson sat quietly in the bar of The Royal Oak. The conversation was stifled, and a couple of pints of Bass and a half-hearted game of darts had failed to improve their mood. By the time they got to double twelve, Shrewsbury had had enough. He retired back to his seat, lit another senior service and took a large swig of his pint of Bass.

"Our main suspects dead" he moped, gone down with those other poor sods to the bottom of the sea.

Brian Paterson had even more reason to feel sombre. Alan Tetley had been one of his best mates, and it was only a few weeks ago that he had been at his wedding, and now his wife, Denise, was almost certainly a very young widow. The wedding had been a pretty decent affair, with the service at the main church in Grimsby, St James, and a

raucous reception at the Humber Royal. Paterson inwardly chuckled as he recalled how he relived himself into the pin cup of the eighteenth at the Grimsby Golf Course, adjacent to the Humber Royal.

Paterson and Tetley had known each other since their schooldays at Wintringham Grammar. They had kept in touch since leaving school, as Paterson had joined the Grimsby constabulary, whilst after a few dead end jobs, Tetley had trained to be a radio operator, and had joined the King of Albania, for his first paid trip at sea.

Paterson and Tetley met up regularly at weekends, usually ending up at the Mecca dance hall eyeing up the local talent. Graham and Alan had sporadically got their leg over with some of the girls at the Mecca, and Alan had eventually met his wife Denise there. Paterson's heart sank as he realised that very shortly, he would be almost certainly be attending the Funeral of his best pal.

National and local media besieged the offices of Kings Trawlers Ltd. The owners of GY 642, King of

Albania, now had to show a forced kind of genuine concern for the crew of the stricken vessel, where as previously they had been happy to hire and fire crew at will, and regarded them, like other trawler owners in the town, as a source of casual labour ! Usually, there was little sentiment in the industry, and being lost at sea was seen as a hazard of the job.

After a couple of weeks, any hope of the King of Albania being found had disappeared. Soon, a procession of funeral and remembrance services would take place throughout the town, and the dark, dank days of January and February did little to bring the area out of its collective depression. The hymn, for those in Peril on the sea, seemed like an impromptu local anthem.

Gradually, the Town returned to normal. However, The King of Albania sinking was the last major tragedy suffered by the industry, as by the end of

1976, the deep-sea fishing industry was already in rapid decline. Iceland had been victorious in its efforts to impose a 200-mile limit, mainly due to its threat to close down a NATO airbase at Keflavik, and, according to some, too conciliatory a stance taken by labour politician John Prescott. Conspiracy theories still existed that the King of Albania had been captured by the Soviet Union, accused of spying, at the height of the cold war. Some even believed the crew had defected and were living a life of luxury in Murmansk!!

Sadly, the more mundane truth was that the vessel had sunk without trace.

Grimsby's trawlers had nowhere to fish and were sold off as oil rig support vessels, or, more often than not sent to the scrap yard. The Fish Docks became a shadow of its former self , the Ice Factory closed down, and the North Wall, once rammed with Trawlers ready to go to sea, had fewer and fewer vessels tied up there, as the number of fishing grounds dwindled.

Pat Hewitt and Denise Tetley's lives slowly returned to normal, although none of their families would ever again go to sea. The brutal murder of Jenny Mann in 1975 was slowly forgotten.

January 2000.

Seventy-Five-year-old Bert Shrewsbury was knackered. He didn't get out much these days but felt obliged to attend the retirement party of his old mucker, Brian Paterson. He didn't really like being in company these days and liked even less the song "Glass of Champagne" by Sailor, which reminded him of the days of the Jenny Mann murder. He even managed to give a speech, which he wheezed and coughed through, trying his best to disguise the effects of his recently diagnosed lung cancer. He had drunk a couple of pints of Bass, as, after all they were in the Royal Oak. The barman tapped Brian Paterson on the shoulder and whispered into his ear. Brian looked gobsmacked as he turned to look at the scruffy looking chap sat in the corner of the pub. He didn't recognise him, and he certainly wasn't part of the retirement party.

Brian slowly approached the guy, who held out his grubby calloused hand, which Paterson shook cautiously. "Good Evening Paterson", he whispered in a recognisable foreign accent. "I think you know me as the Icelandic" Paterson quickly released his hand and looked over to where Shrewsbury was sitting. The commotion surrounding the occupant could only mean one thing. Bert Shrewsbury was dead.

So, there it is. I think it ended abruptly due to me running out of the number of the permitted words for the competition.

CHAPTER 4.

Strangely, Grimsby had two main shopping areas, Uptown and Downtown, but I was never quite sure which was which! The Freeman Street area was most prominent up to the 1970's, and its decline mirrored the fall of the fishing industry. A large indoor market, owned by the Freemen of the town used to be heaving, and had wonderfully named stalls, such as "Mad Harry's" and the legendary "Pea Bung" fish and chip shop and cafe. The Pea Bung still exists. There was also Rayners, which was a record/electrical/furniture store. You could listen to record in the listening booths, and I think I bought my first single, David Bowies "laughing gnome" from there. My cousins Steve and Julie had got some Disney story records there, which I wanted. Derek thought them to expensive at 15/-, so I got a music for pleasure

Mary Poppins single, a spoonful of sugar, which I definitely didn't want.

Other outlets such as Marks and Spencer, Woolworth's and Burton migrated to the other, more modern shopping centre, known by many as Victoria Street. (I wonder how many thoroughfares, buildings and urban conurbations celebrate the reign of the diminutive sovereign!).

There was also a fair smattering of well-respected local companies mingling with the big boys. Albert Gaits, the Stationer, Gough and Davy, music shop, which also sold records; Al Capone on 12 inch by Prince Buster was one of my purchases there.

Chambers, I seem to think, was a coffee shop come delicatessen, and the smell of freshly ground beans wafted around the Old Market Place.

Lawson and Stockdales, near Woolies, competed with Chambers on the coffee aroma front, whilst the Odeon (ex-Savoy/Gaumont, /latterly Focus) showed the latest films. There was a statue of a girl with a tennis racquet on the roof, which was a bit odd.

Nowadays, it serves the latest Burgers, as its owned by a McDonald's franchise.

Dad used to like taking me to the pictures, but usually to see films HE wanted to see. Consequently, rather than the latest Disney release, such as Robin Hood and The Aristocrats, I was watching The Battle of Britain , Waterloo and Michael Caine as an upper class soldier in Zulu. I eagerly awaited the ice cream interval. Incidentally, I share the same birthday as Michael Caine,(and Jasper Carrot).

Down at Limber Vale, I was slowly growing up. I was allowed to visit Nielsens supermarket, to purchase shopping on mums list. There was often a note, and one item was a blue box, the contents of which puzzled me. I later discovered it was a box of tampons. Mum also worked for Mr

Nielsen, in the "beer off", and was required to carry the till takings home in a carrier bag on the walk home!

After visiting Nielsens, I often would nip into Lawrence's newsagents for a quarter of cola cubes, or a 10p mixture of penny sweets. Black Jack's and Fruit Salads were 2 for ½ a penny, so you got loads for 10p. It was here I would also get Dads regular order: - ½ oz. of Old Holborn tobacco, a packet of green Rizla papers and a box of filter tips. Dad would assiduously role his fags of a night, before going down dock. He would turn home early in the morning , smelling faintly of fish, and often with a few fillets of haddock. He would tell me the trawlers he'd been working on, some with romantic sounding names like Northern Jewel, others with a historical slant, such as Lord Jellicoe, and Z boats, which i think were Belgian. Scrobs, were Icelandic Boats. He also would regail stories of some of his fellow lumpers,. One I recall was a chap called

Donkersloot, who allegedly had guarded the beast of Belsen after the war.

At Smith's Ideal Fisheries, on Yarborough Rd, Mr Harry Smith had a couple of USP's.

One, he fried Crinkle Cut Chips, and two, he fried customer's own fish. This meant that Dad, who received free fish as part of his job, could send us to the Chippy on a Saturday, get his Haddock or Monkfish deep fried by Mr Smith, and we all had Fish and Chips for Dinner. (Definitely not LUNCH). Year's later I visited Smiths Ideal Fisheries and winced as Harry Smith struggled valiantly to slice a pizza, as he tried to keep up with the times. I think he retired shortly afterwards to ride his BMW motorcycle around Lincolnshire.

Lunch didn't exist in Limber Vale circa 1973. We also had Pudding. Sweet was a group singing Blockbuster and Ballroom Blitz.

Vesta meals for 2 were eked out to feed 5, gravy, custard and mash (but not sugar) came in lumps, and Al dente might as well have been a brand of toothpaste! Mums cooking led something to be desired, and the smell of burning pan handles was not uncommon.

In those days, there was no McDonald's, KFC, or Pizza take outs (I didn't know what a Pizza was until 1980!), Chinese takeaways were very limited, I remember one of the first opening on Cromwell Road opposite Grand ways. Wimpy was an occasional treat!

Every year, one of the biggest events in Grimsby was the Hospitals Gala, at People's Park. There was bingo stalls, live bands, beer tents, and a spectacular show, often a man diving off an impossibly high diving board into an impossibly shallow pool that was on fire, with a tiger swimming around, whilst someone from the White helmet cycle display team jumped over the pool. (maybe I'm exaggerating a little). The Bay

City Rollers probably blasted out from the loudspeakers.

Chapter 5.

I was now attending Yarborough Middle School, on Central Parade.

This meant that pupils from Worsley and Yarborough Junior Schools joined, but, bizarrely the Boys and Girls separated into different buildings, and never the twain would meet.

I look back at my time at Yarborough as the happiest schooldays of my life, and we had some great teachers and a great spirit. There was a mixture of kids from the nearby large council estate (the Yarborough kids), and others from the houses in around Yarborough Rd (the Worsley kids).

We were divided into 4 houses, Drake (Red), Nelson (Green), Livingstone (Yellow), and Scott (blue). In the school Hall, where a classical tune was played every day before assembly, a large points board with movable shields indicated the house points for the week. I think there was a cup for each term. My favourite assembly tune was "when a Knight won his spurs ", by Vaughan-Williams.

The Hall also doubled up as an impromptu cinema for the school film club, where Mr Heelas would show a Norman Wisdom classic, or one of Alistair Sims "St Trinians" films, on his super 8 projector. Smokers sat on the left! We also had a weekly Subbuteo league in the hall. For some reason my team was Celtic (I had no Catholic allegiance, I think I liked the kit colour when I bought it from Bradley's toy shop on Yarborough Rd, which was next to Smiths Ideal Fisheries.

I can remember most of the teachers, my first was recently qualified and was a bit of an eccentric , Mr Williams I don't think he had quite anticipated what teaching a class full of boys would involve, and he did get a fair bit of ribbing from those in his class, and whilst he was on playground duty. Many of the teachers at the school were quite sporty, so on such days when teachers v pupils events occurred, Mr Williams lack of sporting prowess tended to be extenuated. However, I do believe in later life he did achieve a sense of sporting respectability, by becoming a local cricket umpire.

When I first went to Yarborough, the Headmaster was a Mr White. Punishment was still old school, and I can remember pupils be wrapped across the knuckles with the "strap", or having a plimsoll liberally applied to their backside. Not long after starting, a new headmaster, Mr Johnson was appointed. He was a genial old schoolteacher, who in his early days at Welholme Infants School had taught my dad.

Sports day was a yearly highlight, and the houses competed in traditional track and field events alongside those other sports day staples such as the sack race, egg and spoon and the wheelbarrow race.

I do remember winning the wheelbarrow race, and another memory was the slow bicycle race. The idea was to actually come last, without falling off. Hence the slowest cyclist won. One year , with my highly polished Hercules Jeep pushbike I decided to enter. Things didn't go too well. I started by going too fast, which appeared to my watching mother to be ideal as I was leading, and she valiantly cheered me on. Too late in the day, I realised I had to slow down, but unfortunately still crossed the line first, which in fact meant I had come last. Mam still thought I had won!

I think Alan Overton won on his Raleigh Chopper, which had a lower centre of gravity and was easier to control at lower speeds. Luckily for me, one of my opponents fell off his bike, and I was elevated from last place to 3rd!

I became a school prefect whilst I was In Mr Birkbeck's class (who I think Mam had a crush on), but once had my prefect privilege removed when I was caught by Mr Whitcombe as a few of us decided to roll ourselves onto some large school curtains in the art room.

There was also a school museum, where pupils could bring items of interest to be placed in the display cabinet. I think most families must still have held onto their WW2 gas masks, as there was always a different pupils families gas mask on display. If you tried one, it smelt horrible.

At the end of our last term at Yarborough, there was an annual school trip to Staithes in North Yorkshire. We travelled down by bus and were accommodated in Nissan huts on what looked like an old POW camp. Staithes is a delightful fishing village, which has become more of a tourist destination than it was in the 1970's. It has a long jetty, ideal for crabbing competitions for the pupils of Yarborough.

I remember a walk near the village of Goathland, later made famous as the setting for the TV series Heartbeat, and a trip to Whitby. Me and a lad called Gary Byatt won a prize of some Caran d'ache crayons after we made a display of items we had gathered during a beachcombing exercise.

At around this time I also bought my first records. (7 inch vinyl's), and I makes me laugh when I hear these celebrities on the radio being interviewed, saying the first record they ever bought was by Jimmy Hendrix or Steeley Dan. Bollocks!. The top ten of records I first bought is as follows –

1. The Laughing Gnome David Bowie.
2. Snoopy v The Red Baron The Hotshots.
3. Monster Mash Bobby Boris Pickett.
4. The Pushbike Song The Mixtures.
5. Ernie BennyHill.
6. Grandad Clive Dunn
7. Band on the Run Wings.
8. Forever Wizard.
9. Merry Xmas Everyone Slade.
10. Blockbuster Sweet.

Chapter 6.

I was never really any good at most sports, although I did enjoy playing them. It was all the more galling as Kev seemed to be good at most sports. I never made it into any of the school's football or cricket teams (I Once got a game of rounders!) but used to watch the School matches when the school day had finished. The best Footballing Alumni of Yarborough school was Kevin Drinkell, who played for Grimsby Town, and the went on to play for Norwich City and Rangers in Scotland, when Graeme Souness was manager. He was in his last year at Yarborough the year I started.

Away from school, there was a large field called the Waterworks, which, from Limber Vale could be accessed via the imaginatively named Waterworks Woods. Most light nights you could always find an impromptu game of football or cricket going on , and anyone could join in. Great games of about 20 a side could be played, often with a Wembley Trophy football, that was as light as feather, would blow in all kinds of directions, and was easily punctured. An elder lad, who I think may have been a thalidomide victim would enthusiastically join in wearing his Man Utd shirt, but would usually end up reffing the game.

Once a year, the Waterworks (owned by Anglian water) would have a massive bonfire and fireworks display, which attracted most of the local families, and kids would let off bangers and spitfires, whilst the younger ones waved sparklers. Health and Safety would have field day today.

At the edge of the woods was a large area of grass land, which we called 7 hills. Here, there where areas where you could do a kind of pushbike scrambling, and try not to fall off as you descended some of the steep hillocks that lay at the west side of the field. Close bye was the St Michaels church hall, where many of us would attend the 1st Littlecoates (St Michaels) cub and, later scout group. Our Necker colour was Red with yellow piping, with a coloured woggle depending on which "six "you belonged too.

A gentlemen who was normally called Les James, entered the proverbial cub scout bat cave once a week, and clad in a beige shirt and a wearing a green beret, would transform into Akela, the Scout Leader.

I got a few badges at Cubs, but for some reason was crap at knots. The Bowline took me ages to perfect, but I could make a meal and swim quite a distance, so I soon had an armful. I suppose I was also a bit weedy when I was at Cubs. I never really enjoyed British Bulldog, which just seemed like a great excuse for a mass scrap, but much preferred musical chairs!

Once a year, we would spend a weekend in a creepy building called Moot Hall in the village of Holton le Moor. It had stuffed animals and a deer's head mounted on the wall, and, not understandably, there was high jinx after lights out, due to Cubs depending to be ghosts or shining their torches onto the head of the deer. We could build a bivouac in the woods, and, more importantly discover that you were supposed to eat cornflakes with cold milk, rather than milk and boiling water, which was the way mam always made it. I made it to sixer of grey six which meant I had a double stripe on my arm.

Eventually, I went into the Scouts, wearing my green beret, a la Frank Spencer, but somehow Scout's never quite matched the Cubs.

Once a month, we attended church parade at St Michael's Church, which no one really enjoyed, but it meant the Reverend Stanley Jackson would visit us at Xmas, and we needed to be on our best behaviour. Mam managed to get a job cleaning the Church, and the church hall, and every Sunday morning, an elderly gentleman called Mr Palmer would cycle to our house and bring mum her £3 wages. We also would have to go help at Littlecoates House, and old folks' home, and help hand out mugs of camp coffee to the lucky residents. I remember once dropping a big pot of pepper, which the cook seemed to be a bit pissed off about, so I never went again.

Another character at St Michael's who was very eccentric, used to take us to Cricket and Football matches "free gratis", and would visit our house and bring me football programmes from matches he had been to.

He once offered to take me and a friend to see an Arsenal match in London, staying overnight. Mam and Dad said no, which, in hindsight may have been the right decision.

He eventually hung himself in the Church Bell Tower, and I do not think he had a CRB check.

Back at home, once a year, a few of us used to hold a jumble sale come fete in an alley way between Alan Freeman (Not the Australian DJ known as "fluff), and Geoffrey Day's houses. This gradually expanded into Ron and Mavis's garden (Geoff's mum and dad), and we raised money for some well-known charities such as the RNLI, but, as a 10year old I had never heard of muscular dystrophy, so had no idea what we were raising cash for.

I remember my Dad making a type of bingo board, where you would push a piece of paper out of a hole with a pencil. The piece of paper would indicate if you had won, (any amount from 10 new pence to 50 new pence), and you would also gain a small splinter in your finger, as Dad's handy work was not of the greatest quality!.

Most years, a photographer from the Grimsby Evening Telegraph would take a picture, and about a week later, an embarrassing photograph of "6 local youngsters" raising £27 for the Blue Cross would appear.

This was not however, the most embarrassing photograph I ever had published in a local newspaper! The annual Cubs Xmas fair held a fancy dress competition.

This was in the days when Dick Emery played a character in drag, called Mandy, whose catch phrase was "ooh you are awful, but I like you ".

For some inexplicable reason, it was decided this was the character I would dress up as, whilst Kevin would go as Worsel Gummidge. Kev won, I came second, and the photographer from the Grimsby News took a picture of me which was published on the front page of the paper.

Mr Whitcombe, Teacher at Yarborough, thought that it was so hilarious that he pinned it onto the class blackboard. I did not really see the funny side! Mam and Dad took us on a week's holiday to Mablethorpe, to aid my recovery.

Chapter 7

Nanna Tilling, mams mam, lived on a large, council estate called Nunsthorpe , which had quite a ropey reputation., but could be reached by catching the No 4 from outside Nielsens, which would change to the 3F on St Michael's Rd, and we would get off at Bonby Grove. We would then make a short walk to No 9 Marton Grove, where Nana and Grandad George Tilling lived. George was not Mams dad, as Nanna had remarried after Albert Bramhill had died of Heart Disease at the ridiculously young age of 48, in 1958. I didn't have much luck with Granddad's, as William North, known as Billy, also died prematurely of Lung Cancer, aged 56. I was one year old. Dad also had a sister, who sadly died in a tragic accident when her nightdress caught alight after she leant over a coal fire. She was 5.

That's enough of being Melancholy!

Trips to Nunthorpe were either by bus or, car. Dad's cars were never flash, and, never expensive, and therefore never reliable. My first memories of going to Nanna's by car was in a Sky Blue 1965 Ford Cortina, Reg HLY 2C. Nanna Tilling's House was quite a large semi-detached council house, that always seemed to be bloody freezing. Occasionally, a paraffin heater would be lit to prevent the windows freezing, but the smell was quite overpowering, and, combined with the constant haze of cigarette smoke, this was quite a health and safety risk. In the corner of the large front room was the TV, which, under no account where we allowed to change the channel. Only George could do that. If we went on Saturday afternoon, we had to be really quiet as Nanna and George would watch the wrestling on World of Sport. The exploits of Mick McManus, Jackie Palo, and Kendo Nagasaki, amongst many others, would be expertly described from Kent Walton, from a provincial venue, such as Rochdale Town Hall. Half Nelson's and submissions would be eagerly lapped up and cheered on, and we had to stay silent until the Football results started to come in. Mam, who could sometimes have a short fuse, would often pipe up "isn't any bugger speaking then", to which Ivy would whisper to her to shut up.

On a Sunday, the requisite viewing was Songs of Praise, where Nan would sing along in a voice that can be best described as painful, and was often followed by a Salad tea, consisting of some tinned ham, pickled beetroot, tinned potatoes and often some of George's home grown radishes. This would be followed by Jelly and Evap (evaporated milk), and rather bizarrely, a slice of brown bread and margarine. I think it was some hangover from the war when food was rationed. There was also a Pye radiogram in the front room, but the only record I ever remember seeing was a Jim Reeves triple LP.

In the late 1970's Nanna and George moved into a group dwelling near the town centre, where the nicotine haze was even denser. They also had a warden.

Chapter 9.

In the seventies, there was not as much TV as there is now. No breakfast TV, Sky, Virgin, Netflix. Even video was in its infancy. TV even shut down, often in the afternoon, and with a rousing rendition of the National Anthem on BBC around

Midnight. We had 4 channels, BBC 1 & 2, Yorkshire and because of Rediffusion, we had Anglia.

Watch with Mother and Play School was Children's TV., with Brian Cant being dually employed as a Play School presenter, and as the narrator of Trumpton and Camberwick Green, voicing classic characters such as Windy Miller, Dr Mopp and Pugh, Pugh, Barney Magrew, Cuthbert, Dibble and Grubb.

The big BBC and ITV rivalry was between Blue Peter and Magpie. We watched Blue Peter. I remember an Elephant capping all over the studio, Valerie Singleton being Headmistress like, and John Noakes showing his arse after he fell out of a Bobsleigh at the Cresta Run.

The thing I remember about magpie was the theme tune, one for sorrow etc., and Susan Stranks was sexier than Lesley Judd.

The biggest world wide TV event in the sixties was the moon landing in July 1969. As a six year old,

I'm not sure it resonated. We had put a man on the moon, and as Neil Armstrong said " That's one small step for man …… " but more importantly, mums lumpy potatoes could be replaced by something else from outer space, SMASH !.

Chapter 10.

Grimsby and Cleethorpes merge along a random border, which in some cases has Grimsby on one side of the street and Cleethorpes on the other. Whereas Grimsby was a no-nonsense working town, Cleethorpes was best known as a 2nd division seaside resort, in reach of day-trippers from the likes of Sheffield, Lincoln and Nottingham. It had no tower, like Blackpool, no Butlins, like the "so bracing", Skegness, and in fact, there aren't really any crashing waves, as the beach is actually lapped by the Humber Estuary rather than the North Sea. It does have a great reputation for Fish and Chips (haddock, NOT Cod), and has two distinct areas. One to the North, often known as the Wonderland Area, and the Southerly area, known as the "boating lake".

As a Child, Wonderland was a great place to visit. It had a rickety "big dipper", Dodgems and A Ghost Train, but by the 1970's, it was rather tired, and soon to be eclipsed by the likes of Alton Towers and Flamingo Land. In recent years it has been the scene of a Sunday Market.

Multiple numbers of arcades led from Wonderland towards the pier, which as well as penny one armed bandits, had horse racing games, penny falls (as seen in tipping point!), and more recently packman and space invaders.

To this day, an iconic big wheel and helter skelter can be found on the beach, opposite the railway station.

In days gone by, the platform would be choc a bloc with trains from Yorkshire, Nottinghamshire and Derbyshire, but these days you will only find the trans Pennine service to Manchester Airport, and the branch line to Barton upon Humber. The succession of refreshment rooms at the station were very imaginatively named the No1, No2 and No 3! 1 & 2 survive.!.

Further along was the iconic Cleethorpes Pier. In its early days, it was much longer than it is now, in fact it must be one of the smallest piers in the country. When I was young, it was known as the Pier Pavilion theatre, where the lower tier of performers would have a short summer season. Lenny the Lion, Bernie Clifton and the Nolan sisters were some of the seasonal stars, whilst much earlier a young Freddie Frinton, who would go onto be a much-loved comic drunk, trod the boards. One of Freddie shows, Dinner for One, is a national institution in Germany, where it is shown every New Year's Eve. Apparently, it holds the record for the most repeated TV show.

Just behind the railway station in Grant St was a large building that I vaguely remember being the Excel ten pin bowling alley but was much better remembered as Bunny's. This was owned by a famous trawler skipper and would attract some of the top names of the day, such as Bruce Forsyth, Danny le Rue, and unfortunately for me Tom O'Connor. Tom was probably not the funniest comedian on the club scene, one of the last of the old school of comedians who performed in a dinner suit, and refrained from bad language and sex The night we had a works Xmas do at Bunny's, circa 1981, Tom was having an "off night ". Me and one or two others walked out and went to Clouds, a local night club. Human league were probably playing, but no baby wanted me.

Past the Cleethorpes Pier, an iconic part of the seafront was called "Ross Castle". It wasn't a Castle, as I don't think any erstwhile invaders ever believed invaded Cleethorpes was the key to conquering Britain, it was just a fancy pile of bricks that had been built as a folly to attract visitors. Its more of a miniature turret with a pair of binoculars at the top to be honest. Not far away is Brighton slipway, where the RNLI boats are launched. The Humber Estuary looks calm, as there are no large waves, but the tides and sand can be treacherous, and many unsuspecting, and at times, idiotic holidaymakers have relied on these boats to rescue them in times of difficulty. Tragically, this could sometimes be too late.

At the Mouth of the Humber, and quite visible from Cleethorpes beach, are two defence forts, the purpose of which was to stretch some submarine proof netting between them, to protect the vitally important ports of Grimsby, Immingham, and Hull, and prevent Gerry sailing up the Humber.

The real names of these iconic buildings were Ross and Haile Sands Forts, but locally some people refer to them as Bert and Ernie.

The other end of Cleethorpes was known as the boating lake end and was thought of as less vulgar than the "wonderland "end. Not surprisingly, it had an exceptionally large boating lake, complete with duck and goose shit around the edge, but, in the post war years, one of the biggest attractions at this end of Cleethorpes was the "Bathing Pool". What a place it was. Lido would have been to posh a word to describe it, but it was a massive outdoor pool, filled with freezing cold sea water, and a mixture of detritus ranging from sweet wrappers to human faeces. All this for a bargain 2 shillings and sixpence! Why go to Lloret de Mar?

Directly opposite the "bathe o" was Cleethorpes premier entertainment venue, "The Winter Gardens". The venue had a few claims to fame. Resident artistes Jack Lawton and Shirley King, an early appearance by the Sex Pistols, Stranglers, Queen (tickets 70p) amongst others (the sensational Alex Harvey Band springs to mind), and latterly the annual Cleethorpes Beer Festival.

However, all these paled into insignificance when compared to the Winter Gardens tour de force, Melody Night. Except no one called it Melody Night. Everyone knew it as the charmingly sophisticated "bags ball". Every Wednesday night hundreds of locals, holidaymakers, foreign seamen and the odd "bag" queued up to pass the all seeing eye of the moustachioed owner, a Scotsman called Jimmy, to enter a strange mixture of Disco, live singing (often Shirley and Jack), alcohol and casual sex. Many Thursday mornings suffered an increase in illness due to the previous nights exploits.

Further along the south end of Cleethorpes, is an area of land that has had several guises over the years. As a child, it was Cleethorpes Zoo, which would probably not be acceptable in these enlightened times, but it did have cages of Chimps, a Tiger, A killer whale at one time, and a large Elephant house, that also had a hippopotamus with its own small paddling pool. When the cost of keeping real animals became too onerous for the owner, some were sent to other zoo's, some died in mysterious circumstances, and all were replaced by plastic versions, along with some fibre glass diplodocus.

No can ever accuse the local council of not promoting the full potential of this attraction.

To be fair, years later, it became Pleasure Island theme park, which comprised of a collection of Flamingo Land cast off's and some performing seals and parrots. Everyone loved it, so much so that it closed down about 5 years ago! However, some of the ex-bags can buy a swanky flat where the Winter Gardens once stood.

At the south end of Cleethorpes, on the border with Humberston, was a Holiday Park called the Beacholme, "the beachy", and a night club, The Flamingo, "the flam". The beachy had an outdoor pool, which was much warmer than the bathing pool, and had a large concert room, where bands that didn't make the Winter Gardens played. It also provided a large venue for Xmas and new year parties, and well-known local band, like the Rumble Band would play there.

The flam was busy on a Saturday night, and I once fell asleep against one of the speakers, so must have been well pissed! I also remember seeing Bernard Manning there, and for his performance refer to that of Tom O'Connor with profanity.

As the Summer of 1976 approached, 9 Limber Vale had a Henry Spencer and Sons, Sold subject to Contract sign in the yard, and Mam had found her dream home at 32 Anderby Drive, on the Willows Estate, or "The Willers".

Derek North, always a bit cautious when spending money, thought £8950 was too much to pay, but Mam must have charmed him, and we were on our way.... The Wurzels had a brand-new Combined Harvester, and we had a brand new house!

Chapter 11.

It felt a bit weird cycling from 9 Limber Vale with my cousin Steve, who lived in St James Avenue, which was just around the corner, and then cycling home from Hereford Comprehensive School to 32 Anderby Drive. I do remember it seemed a hell of a long way, although just to be clear, I wasn't biking back from Hereford, which is about 150 miles away from Grimsby. Hereford school, was named after Hereford Avenue, which it bordered, although its entrance was down Westward Ho, previously known as Ely Rd!. Due to probable confusion about street names, Herford Comprehensive is now known as Ormiston Academy, and the old school has been rebuilt to look like a futuristic space ship, or something off an ELO album

Going back to Cousin Steve, I was quite envious of him when I was young. His Dad, Uncle John, was a skipper on Deep Sea Trawlers, who, like many of those who had lots of money, with very little time to spend it, would spend like, to quote my mam, "a man with no arms".

Consequently, Steve, and his sister Julie would always have the best new toys and bikes, whilst we, like many others, had to make do with cheaper versions, and sometimes second-hand stuff. Steve would have the all singing, all dancing Subbuteo world cup edition, whilst I had the Club edition, which was basically the Subbuteo version of Blundell Pk. Steve also had a Raleigh Chopper.

Uncle John also had a penchant for new cars, and whilst my Dad would have an unreliable 1970 Vauxhall Viva (Green TOC 340H), John would often have a new Vauxhall Victor, VX 4/90, and one of the earlier Toyota Models, a Crown Custom. He also had the Citroen with the hydraulic suspension, and a rotary engine Mazda. Sadly, in years to come John would end up as a Taxi Driver in an ageing Rover.

So, back to the ride back from Herford. By passing the Trawl Pub, I cycled down GT Coates Rd, which seemed to go on forever, and had some rather smart houses, Passing St Michaels church, scene of earlier Cub Church Parades, I then crossed the River Freshney. It is only a small stream really, and quite often clogged with weeds, but on this particular day in May 1976, metaphorically it was like crossing the Bosporus, as I left one life and embarked on another.

Anyway, enough of that Bullshit! Shortly after the bridge, two large estates emerged on either side of Gt Coates Rd. One, called Wybers Wood, was exclusively private housing, and was still being completed, and the other, ". The Willers"!

The Willows estate actually was 2 separate estates, if you believed my Mam. There was the Private part, and the Council part, and God forbid if you didn't preface where you lived by saying "we live on the private/posh side of the Willows"! Our private house, 32 Anderby Drive, had all mod cons. A garage, downstairs toilet, central heating, a telephone (Healing 3822), and bizarrely a pigeon loft. The reason for this avian abode was the previous owner of the house, raced pigeons, and for a few weeks after we moved in, the pigeons remained. Presumably, Mr Thomas was having a "des- res" pigeon loft built at his new house, on the Wybers (as Wybers Wood inevitably became known as, for who wanted to go to the extra effort of having to say two words when one was more than adequate).

Derek North was not having a phone. There was no need when there was a perfectly vandalised phone box nearby. Maureen North won the argument, and the two-tone green GPO handset remained., (Healing 3822).Derek's shock at the phone bills would only last until Xmas! When a Child is born by Johnny Mathis was No1.

Everything on the estate was new. I had grown accustomed to the area off Yarborough Rd, and knew the area well, and knew all the street names and alleyways therein. The Willows was totally fresh territory. New roads, many with the attractive sounding Service Rd 1,2.3 etc., and unfamiliar shops in a precinct, rather than on a main road. True, the same types of shops existed, but these were unfamiliar incarnations of those down Yarborough Rd.

There was a Fish and Chip shop, but I can't recall its name, Fenwick's newsagents,(Fenny's) which did not seem to have the same homely feel as Lawrence's or Horridge's, and whose owner had a glass eye, a Tate's Supermarket, and a Spar shop, but the precinct had a rather hollow atmosphere. There was also a large estate pub, called " The Valiant", owned by Courage Brewery, which honoured the memory of Valiant heroes, such as Capt. Scott, Edmund Hilary and Leonard Cheshire, all of whom presumably grew up on the Willows Estate. (This would have been quite a feat, as the estate wasn't built until the late 1960's! It was run by a man called Derek, and his wife, who if I remember correctly had a hairstyle modelled on Elsa Lanchester in the Bride of Frankenstein.

Back at 32 Anderby, The Norths were settling in slowly. In Mams case really slowly, as she eventually settled down in 1997! Not long after moving in, the House was up for sale again, as Mam was fed up being stuck in the middle of nowhere! (The Willows and Wybers probably had a population of around 4,000, was on two main bus routes into Town, and was about a mile away from Yarborough Rd! The move back to Yarborough Rd never materialized. I think Derek put his foot down! A la Mrs Webster story. I was still attending Hereford Comprehensive, cycling on my Second Hand Raleigh Sirocco, whilst all the locals went to the newer, trendier Whitgift Comprehensive on the Willows Est (Not to be confused with the exclusive Whitgift School near the Oval Cricket Ground in Surrey).

Whitgift was the first school in Grimsby designed exclusively as a Comprehensive and was actually at the end of Crosland Road. This was named after the MP for Great Grimsby, Charles Anthony Raven Crosland ex paratrooper and Oxford don, and therefore an ideal person to represent the working-class folk of a large fishing port in Lincolnshire. Crosland, however, was a leading light in the abolition of the 11 plus, and the end of Grammar schools. I think his ideology has since disappeared. However, as a flagship Comprehensive, Whitgift had modern facilities, including a large swimming pool and unbelievably a Cinema! It also had a less traditional approach to School uniform. Whereas my Uniform for Hereford consisted of the traditional badged blazer (a phoenix rising from the ashes, and a green and yellow tie), the inmates of Whitgift wore a turquoise coloured turtleneck jumper and a blue Harrington jacket! Bizarrely, the head teachers (Headmaster Mr William Baines), all wore the old fashioned cloaks and mortar boards. Grange Hill meets Wacko.

Still getting used to my new surroundings, I decided to earn some income by getting a paper round. However, as I had decided that Fennies may have been a bit brutal for an introduction to employment, I reverted back to my old stomping ground of Yarborough Rd, and became gainfully employed as a Sunday Paper delivery boy, courtesy of Horridge's newsagents, on the corner of Yarborough and Yarrow Road. It was also a stone's throw from where my educational journey started, Worsley Infants School. It was a tiny shop by today's standards, and Mr and Mrs Horridge were a genial old couple who lived in the house adjoining the shop. Mr Horridge wore glasses, one side of which was blacked out. Visual imperfection seemed to be a trait of local newsagents

So, one Sunday in the summer of 1976, I set of with a guy called Duncan, to deliver Sunday newspapers, to, would you believe, the Willers! As a child of a Grimsby Lumper, the only Sunday Newspaper I ever saw was the Sunday People, or the News of the World, which Nanna North used to read!

I was therefore rather taken aback by the size of the Sunday Times, Telegraph and Observer, and how bloody difficult it was to fold and push through a letter box without ripping the pages. And they made the paper bag weigh a ton! Eventually, I graduated to an evening delivery boy (Grimsby Evening Telegraph), whose Friday night edition included a property guide, and was therefore heavier than normal. There was also a Saturday Sports Telegraph, that contained a Hot off the press report of GTFC's latest game, written by a journalist called Roy Line. The other report, from the Scunthorpe United game, was written by Tom Taylor, whose son Graham became famous at Watford, before managing England. My first evening round, it snowed, I lost my delivery list, and some residents of the Church Meadows didn't get their Telegraph. I got a packet of spangles from Mr Horridge for my efforts.

By the time September 1976 came round, I had spent my first summer on The Willers! I had encountered one or two of the locals and be friended a couple of lads called Gary and Tim, and started playing a few impromptu games of cricket on the Whitgift school field. Gary thought of himself as a Caucasian Andy Roberts, but somehow a tennis ball didn't pose as much threat as a heavy cork ball. It was great seeing him seethe when you hit him for four!

Talking of Cricket, it was during this summer that I attended my first Test Match. The trip was organised courtesy of the aforementioned eccentric who had ended his days in the belfry of St Michaels church, and I remember my Dad , Kev and I boarding a Cabby Cars minibus , along with some other cubs and their dads. I Don't think women liked cricket in 1976. We went to see such greats as Gordon Greenidge, Viv Richards and Andy Roberts, whilst England boasted stars such as Alan Knott and Derek Underwood. However, it was an grey haired, bespectacled cricketer, nearing retirement, who stole the glory. David Steele, scored as Century, became BBC Sports Personality of the Year, but never played for England again. Very unusual for England selectors to make a controversial decision. Many years later, I had a photo opportunity, when the legendary Gordon Greenidge played in a charity game at Cleethorpes. The guy taking the photo, Bob, got so excited, that he only managed to take a picture of mine and Gordon's feet.

Chapter 12.

The long hot summer of 1976 was in decline, Dancing Queen was No.1, and a nervous 13 year old sat alone in the house room of Campbell House, Whigift School. I had met Mr James, Housemaster, who many years later I would call Mike, (even by the progressive standards of Whigift Comprehensive, calling a teacher by his first name would certainly attain the dubious distinction of trip to Royce 3, for a spot of detention). Suddenly, a stream of casually attired pupils entered the room, and a kid called Steve Cook, gave a re -assuring, "who the F**k are you". My first day as a member of 3F3, (Year 3, Fast, 3rd Level) had begun. Unbelievably, the streams were designated as F (Fast), M (Medium) and S (Slow). The slow kids never stood a chance!

As I mentioned, I was in Campbell House , whose colour was Orange, and we were in the West side of the school, along with Royce (Black), Macadam (Brown), and Newcomen (Purple). On the East side of the school, were 4 more houses Brunel (Blue), Stephenson (Yellow), Telford (Red) and

Harrison (Green). For the purposes of sexual equality, the school kitchen was named after aviator, Amy Johnson!

I always thought it was quite odd that the houses were all named after famous engineers, except mine, which was named after a manufacturer of soup and meatballs! Maybe the painting of Bluebird in the locker room WAS there for a reason.

As in most schools, the Subjects you enjoyed often coincided with how much you liked the teacher (or more importantly how good they were at teaching), which is why I seemed to enjoy Chemistry, taught by the enthusiastic Mr Ibbotson, whilst History passed me by, as I can't even remember who taught me . (This was quite sad, as I now really enjoy History).

Another aide to my education was my Dad's tea-time quizzes. If Dad was at the tea table (and this wasn't due to him dividing his time between more than one household, but the fact that he was usually in bed before his night down at the pontoon on the Fish Dock), he would go around the table asking us all a question. The winner didn't have to do the washing-up. Strangely, Dad won most nights.

Before Christmas 1976 was upon us, I had a new set of friends and acquaintances, and in the imaginary Film "Willers Xmas, 1976* the cast was as follows.

Future Best Man/Domino Partner -   Darren "Mars Bar" Love.

Budding Failed Actor   Tim
Gallagher

Whatever happened ?   Gary
Ramsden

Do I look like John Lennon ?   Paddy
Chapman

Posh Kid who became a dentist   Steve
Foley

Steve Cram lookalike/sounds like   Steve
Crampin

Drama Partner   Mark
Flello

Budgie   Mark
Sylvester

Obligatory Girls   Jill
Doyley, Adele Landymore, Sally Moore.

Directed by Monyeen Blakey
Produced by Len Morter.

Len Morter was a rather unconventional teacher. Not a native of Grimsby, he doubled up being an English teacher with being manager of the Whitgift Film Theatre. One night, I remember me and Tim Gallagher, hanging around the exit door of the theatre while the original version of "The Texas Chainsaw Massacre" was playing, trying to hear the adolescent screams of the victims as Leather face butchered them with his chainsaw. That may have partly explained my interest in classic horror films, further expanded by an xmas present of "A pictorial history of Horror Movies ", and a penchant for dropping the phrase " Grand Guiginol" into a conversation, without knowing what it meant.

Not long after, a controversial adaptation of a 17TH Century play, 'Tis a pity she's a whore, was playing, which contained scenes of full-frontal nudity. Suddenly, me and my mates developed an uncharacteristic interest in the John Ford play. After badgering poor old Len, he agreed to let us in the Theatre at the interval, so we could witness the nude scenes. Strangely, our interest in the play soon evaporated once our teenage nudity fascination had been sated.

At around the same time, Len put on a fantastic Mel Brooks Double Bill, of The Producers and Young Frankenstein which I went to with "Posh kid who became a dentist", which we thought was hilarious. Whilst we were singing along to "Springtime for Hitler" and guffawing at Marty Feldman's Igor's " Abbie Normal" gag, my old man, and Mrs Foley (Steve's Mam) where getting more agitated as they waited in the foyer, as the show over ran for about 90 Minutes . Thanks Gene Wilder.

1977, Silver Jubilee year. Street Parties, The Queen on tour, Sex Pistols and a trip to Boot in Eskdale courtesy of Whitgift Youth Club. That turned out to be quite eventful!. Anderby Drive organised a "Peter Pan " themed street party, Dad went as a pirate, and Kev dressed as a crocodile. Even little Darren, Had a small role as a lost boy, but it was a non speaking part, as he was extremely shy. . On the Wybers, The Jubilee pub opened.

I, on the other hand, felt the best way to enjoy the festivities was to visit the Lake District with some of my school mates, and those from a rival school, Western. The TA also came along for a laugh. Harry Collett, a gregarious Yorkshire man, who enjoyed fell running, and in later life gave guided ghost walks of Whitby, was the Youth Club leader responsible for organising the event.

Originally, I was due to go on a trip on the Rhine in Germany, but, as more people I knew were going to the Lakes, I went see Mr Duckworth, got my Deposit, and handed the cash over to Harry, to go on a trip of a lifetime to Boot. Boot Camp, here we come.

So, in early June 1977, we boarded a coach outside Whitgift Youth club, and, after picking up some kids we didn't know (including GIRLS), from another esteemed local establishment, Western School, we departed for the lakes.

Little happened to start with, apart from Ian Morton falling in the cesspit, and the majority of the camp nicking the weeks supply of Mars Bars. Some romantic liaisons also began to flourish between the Whitgift boys and The Western Girls (so well known that the Pet Shop boys later wrote a song about it) But metaphorically speaking, the week began to go a bit down hill, the day we decided to ascend Scafell. The TA members who had come along for the ride, marched to a site halfway up Scafell, were we would camp for the night. The next day, a seemingly simple task of cooking breakfast, went tits up. I had shared a tent with Paul Johnson, and we set up the Calor gas stove on a slope, fully exposed to the prevailing wind. The first two scrambled eggs ended up on the slopes of Scafell, as the Calor stove blew over. After successfully anchoring down the stove, the next egg was cooking perfectly, when a rogue gust of wind blew the tent opening flap into the stove, and the tent was suddenly on fire.

Things could only get better, but sadly they didn't!. After a day out on the rickety Eskdale to Ravenglass railway (by the way, there's bugger all at Ravenglass), when the highlight of the day was relieving the local petrol station of most of its sets of Top Trump cards, Jubilee day arrived, and to celebrate, the TA, organised a canoeing trip on Wast Water, the deepest and coldest Lake in Cumbria.

Thing was, most of had never canoed in our lives. It all started as a bit of fun when we all had to run across the line of canoes without falling in. After that lark, someone decided we ought to canoe over to the other side of a rather choppy lake. This I did with a certain amount of trepidation, and promptly did a semi Eskimo roll, and fell in. It was absolutely freezing. Undaunted, I remounted (probably not the correct term), and about a Nano second later fell in again. About 2 hours later, I awoke in Whitehaven General, suffering from severe hypothermia, dressed in a large knitted jumper, that had been donated by some worried hikers. In the bay next to me was the motorcyclist, that the speeding Land Rover, driven by the TA, had knocked down whilst transporting me to hospital. He had broke his leg.

It seems I was probably never told how close to drowning I had been, and Mam freaked out a bit when she heard.

Shortly after this escapade, Paul Johnson emigrated to South Africa, and Harry Collett retired to his Whitby Ghost Walks. I'm sure it just coincidence. I think I got a consolation snog from one of the Western girls on the coach home as Mr Blue Sky played on the coach radio.

Back at Whitgift, Len Morter, had asked for volunteers to supply material for a new school magazine. This went well for a couple of editions, I wrote some crappy poems, Sally Moore was the movie reviewer, who had a schoolgirl crush on Warren Beatty, and I remember Paddy Chapman and his rather nerdy mate, Karl Sims, writing some erstwhile piece on the brilliance of Be Bop deluxe. However, the crowning glory of the mag came around issue 3. Darren Love, under the pseudonym ARS Edwards, wrote a spoof interview with a well known teacher. One question was "Which person in the world would you most like to meet"?, to which the alleged answer was "My Father". The said teacher appeared not to see the funny side of his questionable parentage, and not long after the unveiling of the edition, Mr B Smith, Deputy head issued a very stern announcement on the school tannoy.

"ANYONE WHO HAS PURCHASED THE SCHOOL MAGAZINE, RETURN IT TO MY OFFICE IMMEDIATELY! ". I reckon Lenny Morter would have got a right rollicking from Headmaster Billy Baines. (Who's brother Brian read the news on Look North).

A rare copy recently sold at a Jackson and Green auction for£2.!.

Chapter 13.

Nowadays, social media is commonplace, news instant, and there are hundreds of TV channels to choose from, most showing absolute garbage. Songs are streamed, and everyone's pet is a potential lassie, Felix or champion the wonder horse.

In the seventies , things were somewhat different. We had 3 TV channels, BBC1, BBC2 and ITV (Yorkshire). Video recorders had just been invented, and towards the end of the seventies , video recorders (a great scrap between VHS and Beta max) started becoming popular. A plethora of Video rental stores grew up in the town, long before the behemoth's of Blockbuster et al, where for the princely sum of £2, you could rent the latest Video release for the night. Take away pizzas were now more popular, so a VHS and a Chicken Calzone was a treat. Occasionally, the VHS tape would snap, and the pizza would be cold by the time we had got the vide recorder working.

Blank tapes could be used, but this required quite a degree of technical ability, and Dads attempts to record the 2:30 from Haydock, would usually result in a screen of horizontal snow, and Dad yelling " Maureen, have you touched the Video recorder ? ". Dads Saturday afternoon entertainment of studiously studying the outcome of his 50p ew Round Robin was buggered.

Talking of which , 70's TV was non-pc. A popular comedy had white and black neighbours trading insults that would make the present day politically correct brigade collapse of asphyxia. Probably the most famous comedy of the Day, Dad's army, may have seemed innocent, but had a un subtle subtext of illegitimate children (Pike, whose father was possibly Sgt Wilson), repressed homosexuality (the vicar and verger) and unhappy marriage (Capt Mainwairing). Another Perry and Croft vehicle, "It Aint half hot mum", had a number of Indian actors, but the main Indian character was a well known English actor, who "blacked" up.

Anyone watching football today, will watch as overpaid prima donnas fall over in agony at the slightest challenge. Watch football in the seventies, players like Norman Hunter, Nobby Stiles and at Grimsby Town Bobby Cumming, had a no nonsense approach, They would try and break an opponents leg, and if they were unlucky, the would be booked. Sending offs hardly ever happened.

Chapter 14.

Around 1978, a couple of things happened. I began to go to more GTFC away games, and became acquainted with alcohol. Maybe the two were Intertwined my first away trips take me to such exotic places as Wigan who's first ever Football League home match at Springfield park was against town, and we also did a trip to Wembley. We were supposed to watch town, and visited prior to a crucial FA Cup game against Wimbledon. Unfortunately the game was cancelled due to rain ,and , after the trip to Wembley, where I took a sneaky **** in the Queens toilet, and lifted the fake FA Cup in the style of Frank McLintock., The coach trip supporters rather bizarrely ended up at Brisbane Rd watching a game between Leyton Orient and Charlton athletic. I can't remember the score but did have a meat pie. Further away visits ensued and I distinctly remember getting kicked up the backside at Crewe Alexandra by some itinerant Man United fans. My experience of unprovoked attacks had a distinct Manchester flavour as I also I also remember getting punched a few times outside Manchester cities ground, main Rd .

Around this time, I also began frequenting a local Tetleys hostelry called The Cricketer's, which was down Littlefield Lane. We used to go in a a room called the green room, which seem to not have a problem with underage schoolboy drinkers. We used to go with a grown up lad called Steve Chrome, who seemed to enjoy our company.

A couple of pints of Lowenbrau, as it sounded trendy, and a few game of pool, and we all felt grown up. I think Steve Marshall was 14 !

Punk was big news. The Sex pistols and the Stranglers had played the Winter Gardens, and the youth club disco, as well as playing some standards, and the odd Northern Soul classic, (The Snake was a staple), reverberated to po-going to The Sound of the Suburbs by The Members. Gaz Sewell, Resident DJ, lived opposite Tim

Gallagher, and later was Resident at Grinders and the Flamingo.

We also went swimming at the school pool on Youth Club nights, but sadly my canoeing lessons came too late. I do remember larking about one night with some girls we quite fancied. Inexplicably, I jumped from the side of the pool onto one of the girls heads, she nearly drowned, and any chance of romance fizzled out.

Chapter 14.

Beer and football seemed to becoming major players. Away trips often involved a few of us travelling in a Fiat 127, driven by Dick Johnson, Tim Gallaghers ex brother in law, whilst listening to Quadropphenia on his cars tape player.(Probably a C120!), and once I remember my dad organising a lift to Barnsley for me and Darren Love, in the back of an old Morris Oxford, being chauffeured by an old guy called Ken Topham.

Ken was an ex jumper, but after retiring helped run a couple of Snooker Halls owned by his son. Kev and I would bike most Sunday afternoons to Garth Lane for a couple of hours of Snooker, a cup of tea (no alcohol allowed), and a Caramac Bar. Kev became quite good at Snooker, but my sporting prowess once again stayed dormant. A couple of other Snooker related issues :- On the register In Mr Grommets tutor group, my name was next to a lad called Dean Reynolds. He was always absent, playing Snooker, and once was the world No8. It didn't last long, the trappings of fame led to too much alcohol and ill health.

Another well known locally player was Mike Hallett, who would sometimes turn up for a game of Snooker at my mate Robin's house on a Sunday. Mike faired a bit better than Dean, and he commentates on Eurosport. Grimsby also became the centre of national interest, due to a by election held whilst the Labour Government of James Callaghan was in deep trouble. Sadly Antony Crosland had dropped down dead, so a crucial by- election ensued. The local labour party pulled a rabbit out of the hat by selecting well-known local TV personality, Austin Mitchell as their candidate, and he scraped through. What I remember, were 2 of the fringe parties. One was called The Sunshine Party, and one the Malcolm Muggeridge Fan Club, which would have been even sillier if the candidate was Tarquin Fintiim Limtbimbin bim lim bim fftang Ole biscuit barrel, as Python and Muggeridge had previous. The fan club got 30 votes.

.

1978 included the World cup from Argentina. Rod Argent, who I thought must have been Argentinian, composed a memorable theme tune for the BBC. Argentina shone, I don't think England qualified. Scotland did, but Allys tartan army were pretty rubbish, although Archie Gemmel scored a memorable goal against The Netherlands.

The 1978 FA cup saw Ipswich beat Arsenal in a bit of a shock, and I got a bit drunk drinking 2 cans of special brew, watching it at a dodgy acquaintance of Tim Gallaghers. At this time, Tim had christened me Spongeboot, on account of the fact I wore some Clarke's polyveldt shoes mam had purchased from Grattans catalogue. She also had stints with Freemans' catalogue, and the Kleeneze brochure, and in 1978 worked in Tates off licence. This was handy for the odd cans of beer (wards Sheffield Bitter)needed to go to parties, often at Sally Moores house, or Great Coates reading room.

It was about this time that once again, I dipped my toe into becoming a thespian. After a successful one night stand playing a character called Carman the Barman in a Len Morter and Monyeen Blakey production, I decided to go with Tim, to a youth acting class, at the Renowned Caxton Theatre in Cleethorpe Rd. This reminds me !. The road in Grimsby, that leads to Cleethorpes is actually called Cleethorpe Rd, (as in singular). There is a convoluted reason for this, which I can't waste valuable time explaining, and, anyway it will spoil the conundrum. If you're interested, ask a local historian.

Anyhow, back to the Caxton's. They were based in a small theatre, creatively named "The Little Theatre", near Riby Square, and after catching the No45 , I alighted with Tim, for an acting master class. After a few Marcel Marceau/Kenny Everett esque attempts to open a door, my dream of an acting career was suddenly shattered, as was the glass chandelier that I managed to smash when moving chairs around the rehearsal room. Would be amateur directors can be miserable bastards, and I was made to feel 2 inches tall. My acting talents were put on the back burner for a few years.

Tim prospered, and eventually started in a film with Sean Bean, and had a bit part in the bill. The last I heard, he was grave digging in Coventry.

Back at Whitgift, it was,Mock exams, my first GCE O Level, and Mam getting frustrated at Paddy Chapman arriving earlier each day to go to school.

" Tony, the little professor is early today" would be just loud enough for Paddy to hear, but he remained steadfast in his exaggerated time keeping.

I would soon be embarking on my last year at Whitgift Comp.

Chapter 15.

So, 1979. Dads 1973 Green Ford Escort had replaced his 1970 Vauxhall Viva, Kev had developed a strange friendship with 2 odd lads called BuBu Stones and John King, whose principal form of entertainment seemed to be jumping off our pigeon shed roof (the name stuck, long after the last pigeon had flown), and smoking coloured Gaulouise cigarettes.

Darren was now 8, and mates with Stephen, who lived next door. They also had a rather vicious looking German Shepherd called Heidi, whose bite was worse than her bark. The games of cricket, that we played down the drive, were often interrupted as one of us would smack one of Dads deliveries into number 34 Anderby. Strangely, Dad never did hit the ball into any prohibited area.!.

I revised extremely hard for my O levels, although the odd trip to " The Cricks", paper rounds, and house parties may have contributed to not getting fantasic grades. I did Okay, and was due to start A levels, in the September.

I did actually apply for 2 jobs however. One as a Laboratory Technician at multi national chemical company Ciba Geigy, who had a very modern, state of the art Lab, and one as a Junior Medical Laboratory Scientific Officer Grade A, at Grimsby General Hospital, Earl St, Grimsby. The lab there looked like a shit hole, compared to Ciba.

A couple of weeks later, dressed in a powder blue jacket with massive lapels, purchased from Ray Allan's, I caught the No16 to town, got caught in a massive downpour, and entered the interview room looking like a drowned rat.

There I was confronted by a pleasant chap called Dennis, and an incomprehensible Scottish Dr, who reminded me of James Robertson Justice from the Doctor in the House and Carry On films. I never understood a word he said, but answered questions using a mixture of answers that included Biology, NHS, Grimsby Town and The Day of the Triffids.

I didn't hold out too much hope. I couldn't understand the questions, I was wet through, and I never have read The Day of the Triffids. Anyway, the lab was a shit hole. A week later, I accepted the job.

A few games of Snooker at Grimsby Leisure centre, the discovery of Vesta Chicken Supreme, a week in a Caravan in Guisborough, and the beginnings of a great season for GTFC, not to mention a week on the dole, and on September 3rd 1979, I entered the doors of Grimsby Pathology Laboratory.

So, the lad who grew up in Grimsby was about to embark on a new adventure. Grimsby, a place whose identity is so confused, it's not surprising it has a questionable reputation. Frustrated

Grimbarians will have all bit their tongues when asked "isn't it in Yorkshire? ". By ignorant half wits.

It was in Lincolnshire, got dragged kicking and screaming into a forced amalgamation with the North Bank of the Humber to form Humberside, which was dissolved after about 30 years. Lincolnshire then did not want us back, so we became NE Lincolnshire. The Post Office still insist we are South Humberside, which was never an official entity in any case.

Independent, a bit rough round the edges, and past its Halcyon days but it's where, in the words of Paul Young, I have laid my hat.

Chapter 16.

Talk about being nervous. I sat in the waiting room , along with a selection of local hypochondriacs, and 4 wide eyed sixteen year olds, who were about to start employment in the Pathology Laboratory, Grimsby General Hospital.

Apart fro me, Niger Walker, Amanda Watson, Jane Gibbons and Carol Campbell sat awaiting for Dennis Bilton to arrive. There was a feint smell of phenol and urine in the air, as Dennis introduced himself, and took us to what was grandly described as his office, but looked more like a broom cupboard at the edge of the Tea room. As I mentioned, the lab was a series of Victorian houses, converted into the Pathology depth, and hence was a rabbit Warren of small rooms, any of which Victor Frankenstein would have felt at home.

Myself and Mandy Watson were told we would be working in a department known as Haematology, and I had not a clue how to spell it, never mind what it entailed. A guy called Mr Lambert, who seemed old as he had just turned 40, was the Chief Medical Laboratory Scientific Officer, and he introduced us to the rest of the Haematology staff. Suddenly, I was in a total alien world, surrounded by a diverse mixture of white coated nerds, talking about subjects which couldn't comprehend and making smutty innuendos which I didn't understand. I was like a rabbit in the headlights, and in one of those rare situations in life when you feel like you might shit yourself.

I then did something stupid. There was another much older girl in the lab, who I think was 18, and I asked her a simple question along the lines of " where shall I hang my lab coat". She glared at me, took a deep breath, and haughtily replied "What you asking me for ". It was a relationship that would continue with this type of jovial informality for the next 30 years.

I was rescued by a friendly face, who had obviously honed in on my look of terror, and was shown the peg to hang my coat. The most terrifying hour of my life so far had ended , but I had to wait until 5:30 pm for the first day to end. I do remember being taking to the staff canteen for my "free "dinner, as under 18's didn't have to pay, and having a massive portion of Shepherds Pie and veg, with stodgy rice pudding. We sat on tables with tablecloths and jugs of water, but did not receive the waitress service reserved for the Consultants Dining Room.

Just before I left to cycle home, at the end of day one, and wandering if I should return for day two, Dennis Bilton asked to see me and Nigel Walker in his office !. What had we done wrong ?. Where we in trouble ?. Dennis closed his office door, and apologetically asked us, "When you turn up in the morning, please wear a tie!". The old Herford phoenix would have to be be raised from the ashes.

So, I cycled home, crossing a bridge on the Boulevard, by passing the Longship pub, under the Haycroft St underpass, and down Crommy *Rd towards the Willows. I had brought a bike from Grandad George , but it was not the sort you could take to Lindsey Roads Cycle Club.

- *Crommy, short for Cromwell.

A few days at Pathology later, and my vocabulary was being inflated with weird words like, Neutrophil, Erythrocyte sedimentation, and Prothrombin, to add to the Grand Guginol of earlier. The word " special", also had a strange derivative. Only men came for a" special" test, and , it involved the unfortunate victim having to walk , like a condemned man, down the mortuary alleyway, past a large window, where he would try and avoid eye contact with the well informed lab staff , to a small gents toilet. If he was lucky, the Chief in Histology wouldn't have just had a fag and some of his home made "liqueur " in there. Some minutes later, the poor chap would emerge from said bog, clutching a pot of semen, usually looking completely embarrassed.

The lab staff gorping at him through the Haematology window would have not aided his relief. One foreign chap got so nervous, he produced a pot full of faeces, and a rather embarrassed colleague had to produce his " Give us a Clue " mime for producing a semen specimen, in his best Lionel Blair style.

I was also attending the Grimsby College of Technology, doing an ONC in Biomedical Sciences, which also included a "night school "session in the Path Lab. I vaguely remember struggling with standard deviation and the t squared test, and that, at night school, Mr Lambert, was a bit of a tyrant. During practical sessions he would deliberately leave out more reagents than you needed, then had you worrying you had missed something out. He often was a sly bugger.

Then Phlebotomy raised its ugly head. This was the art of collecting venous blood samples, first time, with a minimum of brusing. On my first day being taught the dark art, I turned the colour of Roses lime cordial, collapsed in a heap, and spent an hour in recovery. A few days later, the revered Haematology Consultant, Dr Gerlis, asked me to help him as he extracted 20ml of blood from a young child. He expertly filled the plastic Gillette syringe, with about 22ml of blood, so that the plunger hovered precariously on the edge of the barrel. As the genial Dr Gerlis passed the said syringe to me, the plunger gave up the ghost, and the syringe was suddenly exanguated. Dr Gerlis wasn't chuffed, and I was wishing the ground would swallow me up. Luckily for me, Dr Gerlis, soon left, and was replaced by a fresh faced chap, with a distinctly un-consultant like manner, and a passing facial resemblance to the wrestler, Adrian Street. Welcome, Dr Kevin Ralph Speed.

After my initial experience in Phlebotomy, my Pathology career was becoming a bit more, shall we say eventful. Here is a list of some of the low lights :-

1. Leaving a tourniquet on a patients arm for half an hour after he spooked me when I stuck the needle in.
2. Immersing tissue sample from patients vasectomy into wax before processing, rendering them useless.
3. Periodically getting a mouthful of blood , when perfecting a technique called mouth pipetting This was banned circa 1982.
4. Getting drunk on a Thursday, coming to work hungover, and having to interrupt a patients venepuncture so I could throw up behind Garth ward. On return, I don't think the patient noticed.
5. Trying to bleed a dead patient.

Many other incidents of varying degree of farce continued, but I was slowly developing into a half competent Junior MLSO. I had also been elected secretary of the Grimsby Health Services branch of the trade union ASTMS, although I don't think I was left wing enough to be militant. We did however organise a coach to London to lobby our local MP's during an NHS strike but many of the members decided it would be a good day to do some shopping down Oxford St. Those that stayed at Westminster were entertained by a partially drunken MP for Louth, Michael Brotherton   on his way to a meeting with some sailors. I do also remember a young NHS office worker, who we nicknamed " Red Ange", who later became the MP for Penistone. At the 2019 election she had defected to the Lib Dems, and lost her seat. More of a Lincolnshire yellowbelly than a fervent Red.

Being Secretary also meant monthly trips to the upstairs room of the Smokers Arms pub, where Brothers and Sisters would debate important issues of the day, such as the annual subscription to the Morning Star, over a couple of pints of Worthy E. (I'll second that, Mr Chairman !).

Drinking alcohol was now becoming a much more regular occurrence, as on Turning 18 in 1981, I could officially drink in the local boozer, the Jubilee Inn, on the Wybers. Also, as part of a long family tradition, I was invited to join the Hainton Recreation Club, on Heneage Rd. Dad had joined in 1954, at 18, and his Dad had also been one of the founder members, so it was a matter of family honour that I joined.

I was summoned to a meeting before the committee, so put on my best bib and tucker, and entered the committee room with some trepidation. The politburo of the Hainton looked me up and down between sips of Whitbread Mild, and one elderly piped up " Are you Billy North's Grandson ", to which I answered yes. I was in. I had a celebratory game of snooker, got a break of 24, and was on top of the world !.

Away from the Hainton, most weeks consisted of a few nights a week in the Jubilee, Saturday in town or " down meggies " and a visit to a local nightclub. Local hostelries visited included The Haven and Lloyd's in Grimsby, followed by a night at Grinders, or if in Cleethorpes, The Dolly , (dolphin) or strides at the lifeboat. The Lifeboat has since been converted to swanky flats, providing a great sea view for those with a few spare quid in the bank . The nightclubs we visited at Cleethorpes were Clouds, Dean's (or JD's- named after that well known Cleethorpes rebel Jimmy Dean), Pier 39, (now the biggest chip shop in the country), and Bunny's, the same place where Tom O'connor had had such a brilliant evening. A Few years later, Me and a mate got escorted out of JD's on account of finding the ELO tribute band a bit shit. The manager who threw us out, Roly Godfrey, used to be our milkman, and mother was mortified .

Bunny's also held a place in my affections for other reasons. The film, Quadrophenia, had led to a bit of a "mod " revival and a few of us became 2nd rate mods. None of us had a vespa, but we did each posses a pair of two tone trousers, and i think Lovey and Ramsden had a two tone jacket. I had a suit, but it was wollen check, on account of mam buying it on " tick" at Lawson and Stockdales. Being a more traditional department store, two tone suits were too vulgar for L&S, so reluctantly, I would wear it for nights out, looking rather out of place amongst the would be Phil Daniels and Stings. Dressed like that, I wouldn't have stood a chance with Lesley Ash !. Also, I was useless at chatting up birds. So one summer night, all my "mod" mates were at Bunny's, and as I sweated profusely in my Lawson's worsted suit, a group of new age "rockers "entered, sarcastically singing "we are the mods", and were obviously looking for a bit of aggro. Discretion, or more like cowardice, is the better part of valour, so we all scarpered and hid in the "dolly" until the Cleethorpes Coast was clear. My mod days were over.

On a particular night , Nov 20th 1984 to be precise, Grimsby Town were away to Everton in the " League " Cup, and miraculously they won 1 0, Paul Wilkinson sending a header past a hapless Neville Southall. More importantly , the Jubilee domino team had an away game in the Market Hotel, (as in Chapter 1), and I was drafted in as reserve. I partnered Darren Love, and somehow managed to win a game of 5&3's without really having a clue what i was doing. 36 years later I'm still playing, but many of the 1984 venues are defunct.

Do you remember these:'
The Longy, (Longship), The social club down
Elsenham Rd, Nags Head/Waterloo, Gunners
Watch, Kent Arms, Albion, Palace Buffet,
Royal Oak, Oak Tree ,The Queens, to name a
few.

My other sporting venture around this time,
was playing football for the Hospital Sports
Under 23's, on a Sunday afternoon. We were
terrible. The local equivalent of
Barnstonworth in Michael Palins ripping
yarns, we would regularly get hammered by
10 goals or more. Most weeks we could
scrape 8 or 9 players, and to cap it all, the
manager, Mark Lister, would often arrive 2
minutes prior to kick off with the kit , which
was sky blue, made from brillo pads, and 2
sizes to small, and damp from the local
laundrette. We seemed to play on
permanently boggy pitches, which
occasionally had cow pats on them, and

therefore would end up lathered in mud and cow dung. My proudest moment was scoring a goal by accidentally dribbling the ball past the opposition keeper and walking it into an empty net a la Terry Curran style.

I also played cricket for the cricketing equivalent of Hospital sports, NDLB CC (National Dock Labour Board), and the Hospitals Midweek 2nd team , Phoenix. I didn't bowl, often batted at No 10, but would willingly umpire and fill in the scorebook. I once scored a 50 against Lout Police, and took a blinding catch at the now defunct Hospital ground, but my sporting prowess barely merited a flicker on the sporting richter scale.

Friendships and relationships were also in a state of flux. Gary Ramsden fell out with us because we wouldn't allow him to get served ahead of us in the Jube , and Tim Gallagher had gone to be a lovey, at the Crouch End

School of Drama. I was now " courting" (as mam would call it), a nurse called Debbie Gray. We met in very un romantic circumstances, as we were both throwing up in the same toilet, at a party in the Nurses Home.

Darren Love and Steve Marshall were also dating nurses, so the six of us ended up on regular nights, which if not in the Jube, could have been in the Bull Ring, The Saxon Arms, or down meggies, ending up at a pizza restaurant down Freeman St.

On a Sunday, the Lads from the Path Lab would head out to Robin Howes House situated down an isolated rd. in Healing. The night usually consisted of being Driven to the Blacksmiths Arms at Rothwell, in the back of a lad called Craig's works van, Drinking 6 pints of Everards Tiger(Craig included), and then playing Snooker at Robins while 1am, whilst listening to his shitty American MoR music. Africa by Toto still haunts me.

A few of us also performed risqué versions of Paul McCartney's Frog Chorus, and Snow White and the Seven Dwarves (some reference to Seven up was mentioned), at the annual Hospital Revue at either the Winter Gardens or The Casablanca club.

On the whole, my formative years were coming to a conclusion. Mates were getting engaged and married, and after dilly dallying for a few years, I followed suit. I married Debbie Gray, on a great day in June 1988. I even hired a Double Decker bus to ferry the Grimsby clan to the Wedding at Burton upon Stather, with a reception at Normanby Hall. It was also memorable for the driver of the Bus. I asked Dad to collect £1 from everyone on the bus for the fare home. Dad had got drunk did his well known Al Jolson and Frank

Sinatra repertoire, and gave the fare money to the driver as a tip !

Me and Deb moved into a house down Corinthian Ave, and The Cricketers became our local. In 1991 Daniel Antony North was born, followed in 1994 by Kieran John.

As I write this, I have been married for 32 years, am semi retired having spent 40 years in Pathology (never quite matching the prank played by a colleague who replaced faeces with chocolate icing, and licked faecal material whilst demonstrating the technique to an aghast trainee), and am a Freeman on the committee of Freeman St Market. I still occasionally watch GTFC, which can be traumatic at times, and the yearly holidays to Norfolk and Mablethorpe have been upgraded to Europe Canada and S Africa but I have remained in the same town and same profession all my life. I once had a record played on National radio when you were asked to submit a song that summed up your Town. I chose " Road to Nowhere" by Talking Heads, which may sound a bit negative. But if you take the road, you'll find a fiercely proud and independent area, that, is down on its luck, and is constantly forgotten by the mandarins beavering away in the Metropolis. Thanks Grim !

Printed in Great Britain
by Amazon

43147476R00078